Rainbow in my Pocket

Rainbow in my Pocket

Written by Terri L. Glimcher
Illustrated by Michael Meister

Contributor: Tammy J. Mackey

Self-publishing partners:
Studio 6 Sense, LLC • studio6sense.com

ISBN: 1492270601
ISBN 13: 978-1492270607

To my beautiful grandchildren:

Nana loves you.

Tomorrow is my first day of school.

I'm as scared as I can be.

Is there anyone else at my new school who will look just like me?

My hair is curly and my skin is brown.
Will there be anyone else like me around?

My daddy is brown and my mommy is light.
In my old neighborhood that was all right.

Now we are in a brand new town.

Is there anyone else like me around?

I tell my mommy that I am scared. She hugs me tight. I know she cares.

She gives me a rainbow on a string. Then I ask her, "What do I do with this thing?"

She said, "Put this in your pocket,
and never forget, we all
come from this rainbow.
On that you can bet!"

8

"No matter the color of our hair, eyes, or skin, from this rainbow we all begin!"

Today is the first day at my new school.
I must remember Mommy's rainbow rule.

Be nice to others, because one thing I know, each one of us comes from the same rainbow.

I run into my class. I'm feeling proud.
I opened the door, and boy it is loud!

As I look around, I begin to see, that everyone here is just as different as me.

Some kids are short and others are tall,
some have black hair, but that's not all.

There's a boy named John and he can't walk,
so we sit on the floor and play with chalk.

Then I sit in the circle and begin to play with Aniyah, Aubree, Tyler and Mae.

I have fun and play all day long.

Then we get ready to sing some songs.

I hold Aniyah's hand. She holds mine too. We sing our good-bye song, and our day is through.

Mommy's at the door at the end of the day.
I tell her my new school was A-Okay!

We walk home feeling happy. Mom holds
my hand tight.

We cook dinner together,
and then fly my kite.

It's the end of the day and I'm off to bed,
Daddy gives me a kiss, on top of my head.

Mommy gives me a hug and turns off my light.
I cuddle with my rainbow and hold it tight.

"Everyone is different and we all should know, each one of us comes from the same rainbow!"

The End

Cut out and color so you too can have a
rainbow in your pocket.

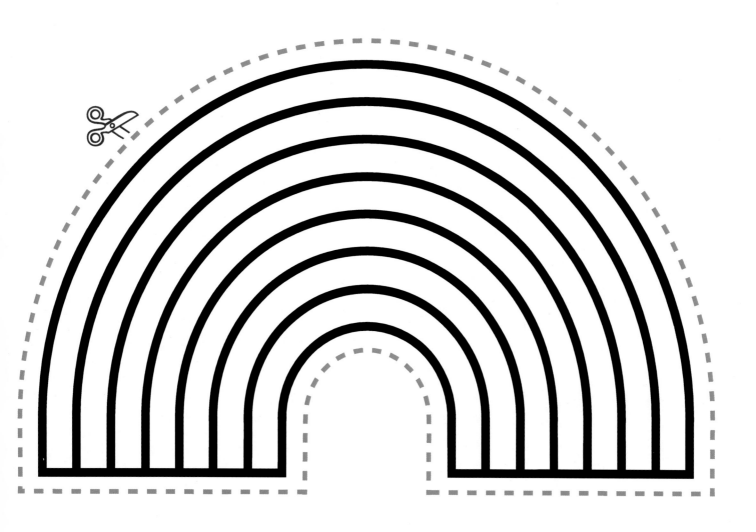

Made in the USA
Columbia, SC
30 June 2021